JESUS AND THE 12 DISCIPLES

CHILDREN'S CHRISTIANITY BOOKS

BABY PROFESSOR

EDUCATION KIDS

Speedy Publishing LLC
40 E. Main St. #1156
Newark, DE 19711
www.speedypublishing.com

Let's learn about Jesus
and His twelve disciples.

Practice writing the
sentences in the
space provided.

"Follow Me, and I will make you become fishers of men." Mark 1:17 (NKJV)

Rewrite the Sentence.

"Follow Me, and I will make you become fishers of men." Mark 1:17 (NKJV)

Rewrite the Sentence.

_____

- - - - - - - - - - - - - - - - -

_____

- - - - - - - - - - - - - - - - -

_____

- - - - - - - - - - - - - - - - -

_____

- - - - - - - - - - - - - - - - -

Jesus picked out his helpers. They are called Disciples.

Rewrite the Sentence.

Jesus picked out his helpers. They are called Disciples.

Rewrite the Sentence.

The twelve
disciples were men
of ordinary means.

Rewrite the Sentence.

The twelve disciples were men of ordinary means.

Rewrite the Sentence.

The disciples played an important part in spreading the word of Jesus.

Rewrite the Sentence.

The disciples played an important part in spreading the word of Jesus.

Rewrite the Sentence.

_____

_____

_____

_____

_____

_____

Judas Iscariot the
betrayer of Jesus
Christ. He was the
treasurer.

Rewrite the Sentence.

Judas Iscariot the betrayer of Jesus Christ. He was the treasurer.

Rewrite the Sentence.

Simon known as Peter. He is most well known disciple of Jesus.

Rewrite the Sentence.

Simon known as Peter. He is most well known disciple of Jesus.

Rewrite the Sentence.

Andrew is most noted for being the first Apostle called by Christ.

Rewrite the Sentence.

Andrew is most
noted for being
the first Apostle
called by Christ.

Rewrite the Sentence.

James was one of the three disciples closest to Jesus.

Rewrite the Sentence.

James was one of the three disciples closest to Jesus.

Rewrite the Sentence.

John the Apostle.
John is known for
writing five books
of The Bible.

Rewrite the Sentence.

_____

- - - - - - - - - - - - - - -

_____

- - - - - - - - - - - - - - -

_____

- - - - - - - - - - - - - - -

_____

John the Apostle.
John is known for
writing five books
of The Bible.

Rewrite the Sentence.

Phillip was slow to recognize Jesus. Phillip died the death of a Christian martyr.

Rewrite the Sentence.

Phillip was slow to recognize Jesus. Phillip died the death of a Christian martyr.

Rewrite the Sentence.

Bartholomew is known for being an honest man.

Rewrite the Sentence.

Bartholomew is known for being an honest man.

Rewrite the Sentence.

Thomas is the one disciple who was not present on the first Easter Sunday.

Rewrite the Sentence.

_____

- -

_____

- -

_____

- -

_____

_____

Thomas is the one disciple who was not present on the first Easter Sunday.

Rewrite the Sentence.

Matthew is recognized for being the first writer of the first Gospel.

Rewrite the Sentence.

Matthew is recognized for being the first writer of the first Gospel.

Rewrite the Sentence.

James is also
known as Saint
James the Less by
the Catholic church.

Rewrite the Sentence.

James is also known as Saint James the Less by the Catholic church.

Rewrite the Sentence.

Thaddeus is also referred to as Saint Jude in the Catholic church.

Rewrite the Sentence.

Thaddeus is also referred to as Saint Jude in the Catholic church.

Rewrite the Sentence.

Simon the zealot
also known as Simon
the Canaanite.

Rewrite the Sentence.

Simon the zealot also known as Simon the Canaanite.

Rewrite the Sentence.

Matthias was
chosen by the eleven
disciples to replace
Judas Iscariot.

Rewrite the Sentence.

Matthias was chosen by the eleven disciples to replace Judas Iscariot.

Rewrite the Sentence.

The disciples with the exception of Judas were made Saints.

Rewrite the Sentence.

_____

- - - - - - - - - - - - - - - - - -

_____

- - - - - - - - - - - - - - - - - -

_____

- - - - - - - - - - - - - - - - - -

_____

The disciples with the exception of Judas were made Saints.

Rewrite the Sentence.

42921875R00024

Made in the USA
Columbia, SC
17 December 2018